The World's Most Popular Sports

Happy House

About Wise & Wide

- A systematic 6-level English reading program based on Lexile® measures
- Diverse and interesting topics chosen from the elementary curriculums of Korea and English speaking western countries
- Well-written books in various forms including fiction stories, descriptive texts, and classics retold
- The informative but original fiction stories grab your interest, leading to the easy and clear understanding of the educational content.
- Improve thinking skills with solid after-reading activities at all levels of the series.

Wise & Wide is a 6-level English reading program that consists of 60 books and each level is systematically divided by Lexile® measures. The Lexile® Framework for Reading is the most popular reading measuring system in American formal education curriculums and many English programs. Over 20 out of 50 states in the U.S. mark Lexile® measures directly on students' final report cards and over 300 well-known publishers adopt and use Lexile® measures.

Experience many kinds of readings written by professional writers from the U.S. and England. They used interesting topics that were carefully chosen after analyzing elementary curriculums from around the world including Korea, the U.S., England, and Australia among many others. Comprehensive after-reading activities including graphic organizers, speaking tasks, and After-reading Tests are ready for you.

Levels in the series and their corresponding Lexile® measures

Level	Lexile® measures	U.S. Grade
Level 1	Below 200L	Pre K - K
Level 2	190L - 400L	Lower Grade 1
Level 3	350L - 530L	Upper Grade 1
Level 4	420L - 650L	Grade 2
Level 5	520L - 940L	Grade 3 - 4
Level 6	830L - 1070L	Grade 5 - 6

* Smart Readers: Wise & Wide level 1 is applicable to the preschool level in the U.S.

* The source of the relationship between Lexile® measures and U.S. school grades: CCSS(Common Core State Standards) FOR ENGLISH LANGUAGE ARTS, APPENDIX A (2012, which is used by 45 states in the U.S.)

Topic List

	Level 1	Level 2	Level 3	Level 4	Level 5	Level 6
Book 1	Science>Biology: The hibernation of animals Story	Science>Biology: Living and nonliving things Story	Science>Biology> Animals & the Environment: Sea otters Story	Environment> Living with nature: The diver & the persimmon tree Story	Science>Biology> Animal: Amazing animals of the Amazon Story	Science>Biology: Germs, transmitted diseases Story
Book 2	Literature> World classics: Aesop's fables Story	Literature> Traditional fairy tale: Old tales about stones Story	Social Studies> Economy: To run a business to make and save money Story	Science>Biology: Plants: Photosynthesis Story	Science>Earth science: Earth's layers,earthquakes, volcanoes, and earth's atmosphere Report	Mathematics> Sequence: The golden ratio & the Fibonacci sequence Story
Book 3	Science>Physics: How shadows are formed Story	Literature> World classics: Peter Pan Story	Science>Scientific technology: Nanobots Story	Literature>Myths: World's creation stories Story	Literature> Legend: The story of King Arthur Story	Literature>Myths: Constellation myths Story
Book 4	Literature> Traditional literature: The Talmud Story	Science>Biology> Animal: Polar bears Story	Science>Biology> Animal: Mountain gorillas Story	Social Studies> Cultural anthropology: Amazing ancient cultures of the world Story	Science> Earth science: Clouds and weather Story	Literature> Human & animals: The friendship between a girl and a horse Story
Book 5	Social Studies> Ethics: Rules in daily life Story	Science>Biology: The five senses Report	Social Studies> Cultural anthropology: Astonishing festivals Report	Art>Music: Stories from two operas Story	Social Studies> World culture & history: The Renaissance Story	Sports> Board sports: Surfing & snowboarding Story
Book 6	Social Studies> World geography & travel: Tourist attractions around the world Story	Science>Biology> Animal: Dinosaurs Story	Science> Astronomy: The solar system Story	Social Studies> People: Three great people who overcame hardships Story	Science>Scientific technology: The wonderful world of robots Report	Art>Music: Composers of the Romantic Era Report
Book 7	Science> Space science: The life of astronauts Report	Social Studies> Cultural anthropology: Mythological monsters from around the world Report	Mathematics> Elementary mathematics: Numbers, measurement, shapes and data Report	Science & Social Studies> Technology & culture: Inventions from around the world Report	Art>Works of art: Famous paintings Report	Social Studies> Human & animals: Animals in action for human Report
Book 8	Social Studies> Cultural anthropology: Various living cultures of the world Story	Art>Music: Instruments in the orchestra Story	Social Studies> Life safety: Learning and using outdoor survival skills Story	Social Studies> History: The California Gold Rush Report	Social Studies & Science> Psychology: Psychology in everyday life Story	Literature> World classics: The Merchant of Venice Story
Book 9	Social Studies> Jobs: Interviews about jobs Report	Science>Scientific technology: Developments in technology in different times Story	Social Studies> Politics>Election: Running for 3rd grade class president Story	Literature> World classics: Stories of Sherlock Holmes Story	Literature> World classics: Adrift in the Pacific Story	Social Studies> History & People: Great world leaders in history Report
Book 10	Literature>Traditional fairy tale: Eastern and Western folk tales on the same theme Story	Sports>Winter sports: Various aspects of some Winter Olympic sports Report	Literature> World classics: Short stories by O. Henry Story	Sports> Ball games: Various aspects of popular ball games Report	Social Studies> History: Famous events that changed world history Report	Art & Social Studies> Art: Stories about the creation, distribution, and preservation of paintings Report

* 10 books in each level will be published.

How to Use
This Book

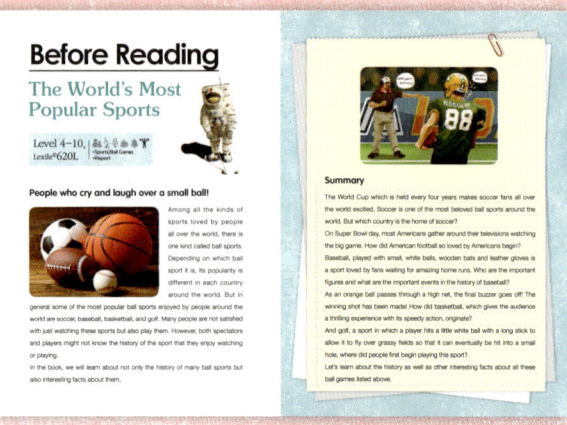

•Before Reading

You can easily find the topic and what kind of story you are about to read.

•The text

All the stories were written by professional writers from the U.S. and England, so you will read authentic and appropriate English sentences and expressions in every book in the series.

•Pop Quiz

Check out right away if you understand what you have just read by solving a pop quiz that checks your comprehension.

•Key Words

The key words and expressions on each page are listed for you to easily study them.

•Aha! Tips

Download free Korean explanations at *www.ihappyhouse.co.kr* for all of the sentences marked with "Aha!". These explain cultural, scientific, and economic knowledge or they deal with aspects of English such as grammatical structures or idiomatic expressions. There are lots of "Aha! Tips" to help you understand the text.

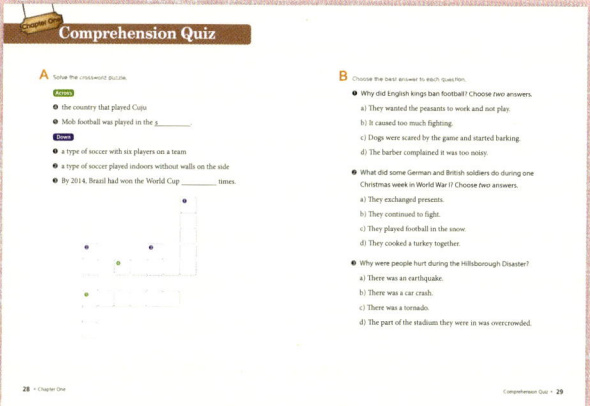

•Comprehension Quiz

After reading one chapter, solve various questions to find out if you fully understand the content.

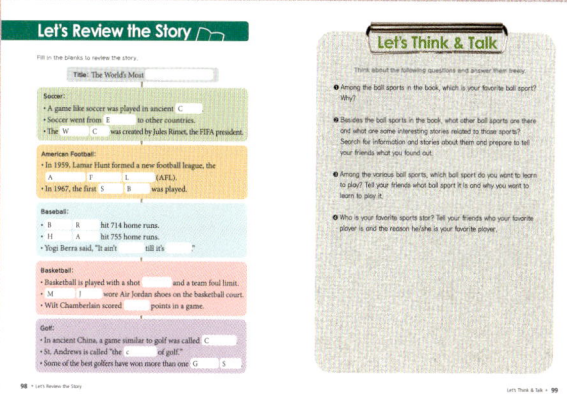

•Let's Review the Story /
•Let's Think & Talk

Fill in the blanks in the organizer to summarize the whole story. Express your own thinking and feelings about the story by answering the questions. You can build up logic and reasoning skills for your essay examinations in the future.

Appendix

Audio CD

In the CD audio book form, the texts are read vividly by American professional voice actors. (MP3 files downloaded for free)

After-reading Test

Solve an additionally provided After-reading Test for each book.

The Korean translation, Answer Keys, a Word Quiz, a Word List, and Aha! Tips for each book

You can download them for free at *www.ihappyhouse.co.kr* or *www.darakwon.co.kr*

Before Reading

The World's Most Popular Sports

Level 4–10,
Lexile®620L

•Sports)Ball Games
•Report

People who cry and laugh over a small ball!

Among all the kinds of sports loved by people all over the world, there is one kind called ball sports. Depending on which ball sport it is, its popularity is different in each country around the world. But in general some of the most popular ball sports enjoyed by people around the world are soccer, baseball, basketball, and golf. Many people are not satisfied with just watching these sports but also play them. However, both spectators and players might not know the history of the sport that they enjoy watching or playing.

In the book, we will learn about not only the history of many ball sports but also interesting facts about them.

Summary

The World Cup which is held every four years makes soccer fans all over the world excited. Soccer is one of the most beloved ball sports around the world. But which country is the home of soccer?

On Super Bowl day, most Americans gather around their televisions watching the big game. How did American football so loved by Americans begin?

Baseball, played with small, white balls, wooden bats and leather gloves is a sport loved by fans waiting for amazing home runs. Who are the important figures and what are the important events in the history of baseball?

As an orange ball passes through a high net, the final buzzer goes off! The winning shot has been made! How did basketball, which gives the audience a thrilling experience with its speedy action, originate?

And golf, a sport in which a player hits a little white ball with a long stick to allow it to fly over grassy fields so that it can eventually be hit into a small hole, where did people first begin playing this sport?

Let's learn about the history as well as other interesting facts about all these ball games listed above.

Contents

The World's Most Popular Sports

The World's Most Popular Sports

The Ball Kicked around the World:

Soccer

It is one of the most popular sports in the world.

More than 250 million people play it.

Players practice moves to bend it like David Beckham or to do the cross over like Cristiano Ronaldo.

What sport is it?

In many countries it's called football.

In some countries, such as the United States and Australia, it's called soccer.

That is because they already have a different game of football.

POP QUIZ.

Mark T for true or F for false.

Australia calls the sport soccer instead of football.   T / F

KEY WORDS

- ball
- kick
- around the world
- popular
- more than
- million

- player
- practice
- bend (bend-bent-bent)
- cross over
- countries
- be called (*cf.* call)

- football
- such as
- that is because
  (*cf.* because)
- already
- different

You might think football started in Brazil or Italy.

Some historians think it was first played in China thousands of years ago!

Back then, they played on a square court with a round ball. This represented yin and yang.

▲ Cuju
(Qian Xuan [Public domain], via Wikimedia Commons)

The Chinese called the game Cuju.

This word means "kick the ball." Even members of the royal palace liked to kick the ball. It became so popular that the Chinese had sports clubs for famous players of Cuju.

KEY WORDS

- might + *Verb*
- think (think-thought-thought)
- historian
- thousands of years
- ago
- back then (*cf.* then)
- square
- court
- represent

- yin and yang
- Chinese
- mean (mean-meant-meant)
- even
- royal palace
- become (become-became-become)
- club
- famous

A few hundred years ago people started playing football in England.

Back then, the working people were called peasants.

They liked to play football because they could play it in the streets.

They called the street games mob football.

Anyone could play.

It didn't matter how many people were on a team.

The only rule was that there were no rules.

Players could kick the ball or kick each other.

▲ mob football
(See page for author [Public domain or Public domain], via Wikimedia Commons)

They could do anything to make a score except kill someone.

You can imagine this game was rough!

KEY WORDS

- a few
- hundred
- peasant
- mob
- anyone
- matter
- be on a team

- rule
- each other (*cf.* each)
- anything
- make a score (make-made-made)(*cf.* score)
- except
- imagine
- rough

The English kings did not like this.

Several kings banned football for the peasants.

They wanted the peasants to work and not play.

Mob football caused too much fighting.

Stray footballs broke windows.

One time a ball flew into a barber shop.

The man in the chair died when the barber's razor slipped.

▲ (See page for author [Public domain or Public domain], via Wikimedia Commons)

However, upper class people decided to let students play it in schools.

Their children liked the game, and perhaps the parents did, too.

So in 1863, a group of eleven schools met.

They formed the Football Association.

They made teams and official rules.

Some of the rules changed over the years.

But some did not.

There are eleven players on a team.

They do not play in the street.

They play on a field called the pitch.

No one may touch the ball with his hands except the goalkeeper.

KEY WORDS

- several
- ban
- cause
- fighting
- stray
- break (break-broke-broken)
- time
- fly (fly-flew-flown)

- barber shop (*cf.* barber)
- die
- razor
- slip
- however
- upper class (*cf.* class)
- decide
- let A + *Verb*

- perhaps
- form
- association
- official
- over the years
- field
- pitch
- goalkeeper

▲ a soccer game between England
and Scotland in 1872
(By William Ralston (1848-1911)
(Scanned from the book Historia del Fútbol)
[Public domain], via Wikimedia Commons)

From 1871 to 1872, fifteen different football clubs from England and Scotland played against each other.

It was the first Football Association Cup.

Then Denmark got interested in football.

Denmark had good players, and they won many games.

They were second only to England.

England won the gold medal in the 1908 and 1912 Olympics.

Denmark won the silver medal.

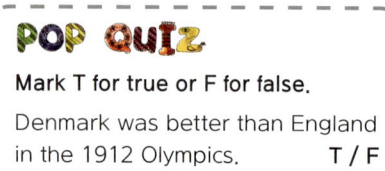

POP QUIZ

Mark T for true or F for false.

Denmark was better than England
in the 1912 Olympics.   T / F

KEY WORDS

- against
- Football Association Cup (*cf.* Cup)
- get interested in (get-got-gotten)

- win (win-won-won)
- second only to (*cf.* second)

16 • Chapter One

In the 1880s, some British working class men left England to find jobs in other countries.

They took the game of football with them.

They worked in the mines and railroads of Spain and Italy.

They taught people how to play football.

Spanish King Alphonse XIII fell in love with the game.

He created the Coronation Cup.

This was a national football tournament in Spain.

The name changed over the years to Copa del Rey (the King's Cup).

The first Italian national championship was played in 1898.

▲ Alphonse XIII
(Christian Franzen [Public domain], via Wikimedia Commons)

KEY WORDS

- British
- working class
- leave (leave-left-left)
- other
- take (take-took-taken)
- mine
- railroad
- teach (teach-taught-taught)
- how to + *Verb*

- Spanish
- fall in love with (fall-fell-fallen)
- create
- Coronation Cup (*cf.* coronation)
- national
- tournament
- Copa del Rey
- championship

Football became more and more popular around the world.

So the sport needed an international group to make rules.

The *Fédération Internationale de Football Association*, or

FIFA, was born in Paris in 1904.

FIFA had members from many countries in Europe.

Football fever was spreading around the world.

It became so popular that even World War I couldn't make

people stop playing.

The week before Christmas, some of the German and British

soldiers stopped fighting.

They gave each other presents.

Then they played some games of football in the snow.

KEY WORDS

- more and more
- international
- Fédération Internationale de Football Association
- be born

- fever
- spread (spread-spread-spread)
- soldier
- present

But there was still no worldwide tournament for football except during the Olympics.

▲ Jules Rimet
(Agence de presse Meurisse
[Public domain, Public domain
or Public domain], via Wikimedia
Commons)

Jules Rimet, the FIFA president, came up with an idea.

His idea was for the World Cup.

He wanted to play it every four years.

He thought it could be almost like the Olympics.

The first World Cup was in Uruguay in 1930.

Uruguay won against Argentina.

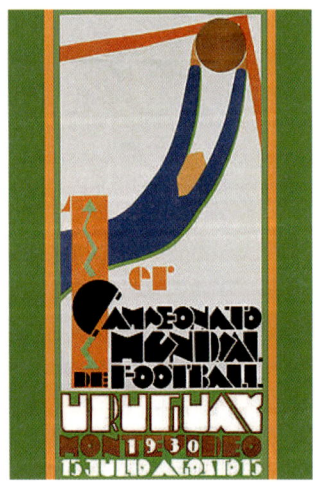

a poster for the first World Cup ▶
(By Guillermo Laborde (1886-1940) [1][2] (FIFA.com)
[Public domain], via Wikimedia Commons)

KEY WORDS

- still
- worldwide
- during
- president

- come up with (come-came-come)
- every
- almost

Then World War II started.

There were no more World Cups for twelve years.

The first World Cup games after the war were held in Brazil.

Brazil built a brand new stadium for the games.

They named it the Maracanã.

It was the largest stadium in the world.

It was big enough to hold 160,000 people. 📖 Aha!

▲ Maracanã
(By Arthur Boppré (Maracanã (Viagem helicóptero))
[CC BY 2.0 (http://creativecommons.org/licenses/by/2.0)],
via Wikimedia Commons)

KEY WORDS

- no more
- be held (*cf.* hold (hold-held-held))
- build (build-built-built)

- brand new
- stadium
- name

- largest
- enough

Surprise!

More than 200,000 people showed up for the game!

Today that is still the largest crowd ever to watch a football game in person.

Brazil was facing off against Uruguay.

The Brazilian fans were excited, but they went home sad.

Their team lost to Uruguay.

However, by 2014, Brazil had won the World Cup five times.

At that time, it was more than any other nation.

One reason Brazil won so many World Cups was due to a tremendous player.

He has many different names.

But most of the world knows him as Pelé.

POP QUIZ

How many times had Brazil won the World Cup by 2014?

ⓐ five   ⓑ seven

KEY WORDS

- surprise
- show up
- crowd
- ever
- in person (cf. person)
- face off
- Brazilian
- fan

- excited
- lose to (lose-lost-lost)
- at that time
- reason
- due to
- tremendous
- know A as B (know-knew-known)

Pelé began playing professional football when he was 15.

He won his first World Cup before he turned 18.

He has the most goals of any player in history.

In 1967, Pelé went to play a game in Lagos, Nigeria.

At that time, Nigeria was at war.

They stopped fighting for 48 hours so the soldiers could watch the game.

In 1999, Pelé was named the FIFA Player of the Century.

▲ Pelé

(By Bilsen, Joop van / Anefo [CC BY-SA 3.0 nl (http://creativecommons.org/licenses/by-sa/3.0/nl/deed.en)], via Wikimedia Commons)

KEY WORDS

- **begin** (begin-began-begun)
- **professional**
- **turn**
- **goal**
- **in history**
- **be at war**
- **be named**
- **century**

In 1970, when Brazil won the World Cup, they were allowed
to keep the trophy.

But in 1983, thieves stole it.

It has never been found.

Now there is a new trophy.

The winning country only has it for a short time to celebrate.

Then, they must return it.

They keep a copy of the trophy.

▲ a picture of the first World Cup trophy

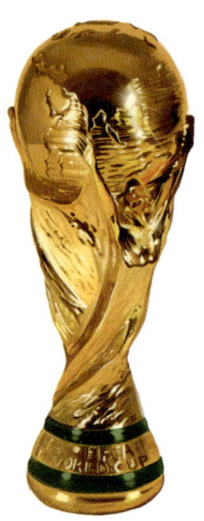

▲ a picture of the present World Cup trophy

Tragedy struck in 1989 at a game in Hillsborough, England.

It is now called the Hillsborough Disaster. 🌐

The match was ready to begin.

Hundreds of fans were still outside the gates.

They wanted to get into the stadium to see the kickoff.

Police opened another gate so more fans could get in.

People rushed into the stadium through the side gate.

It led directly to a part of the stadium that was already full.

POP QUIZ

How long may the winning country keep the World Cup trophy?

ⓐ As long as it wants because it is special.
ⓑ It keeps it only a short while and then it keeps a copy.

KEY WORDS

- tragedy
- strike (strike-stroke-stricken)
- disaster
- be ready to + Verb
- hundreds of

- outside
- get into
- kickoff
- another
- rush

- through
- lead (lead-led-led)
- directly
- full

▲ the memorial for the Hillsborough Disaster
(Superbfc at the English language Wikipedia
[GFDL (http://www.gnu.org/copyleft/fdl.html) or
CC-BY-SA-3.0 (http://creativecommons.org/licenses/
by-sa/3.0/)], via Wikimedia Commons)

Police could not direct the fans safely to their seats. People ran into the overcrowded section. Sadly, 96 fans were crushed to death. Over 400 were injured. Years later, in 2016, the families of the victims received justice.

In a trial, the police admitted they made a mistake.

After the tragedy, FIFA made new rules about stadium safety.

They want to keep the players and the fans safe at games.

KEY WORDS

- direct
- safely
- seat
- overcrowded
- section
- sadly
- be crushed to death
- be injured
- victim

- receive
- justice
- trial
- admit
- make a mistake
- about
- safety
- type
- arena soccer (cf. arena)

- futsal
- indoors
- without
- beach soccer
- crab soccer
- have to + Verb
- crab walk
- certainly
- whatever

Now there are many different types of this sport.

In America, arena soccer is played in an arena with walls on the side.

It is played with six players on a team.

In Europe, futsal is played indoors without walls on the side.

There are five players on each team.

Beach soccer is played in the sand.

▲ arena soccer(a game in which players can kick the ball against the walls around the indoor field)

(By Dravecky (Own work) [CC BY-SA 3.0 (http://creativecommons.org/licenses/by-sa/3.0)], via Wikimedia Commons)

▲ crab soccer

Crab soccer is a game played by children.

They have to play it while they do a crab walk.

Doesn't that sound fun?

One can certainly say that whatever its name is, it is the ball kicked around the world.

Chapter One

Comprehension Quiz

A Solve the crossword puzzle.

❹ the country that played Cuju

❺ Mob football was played in the s_____.

❶ a type of soccer with six players on a team

❷ a type of soccer played indoors without walls on the side

❸ By 2014, Brazil had won the World Cup _____ times.

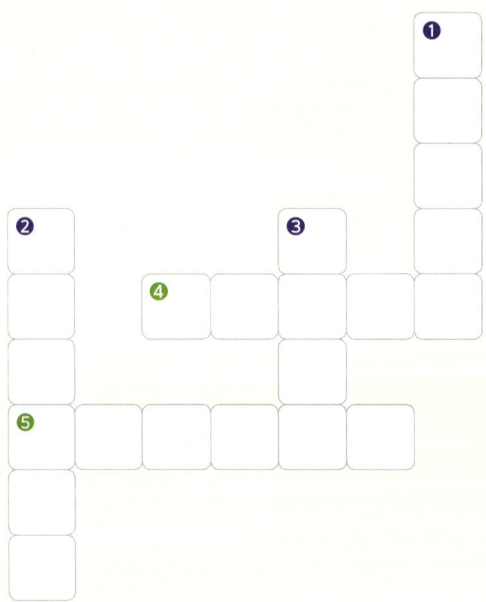

B Choose the best answer to each question.

❶ Why did English kings ban football? Choose *two* answers.

a) They wanted the peasants to work and not play.

b) It caused too much fighting.

c) Dogs were scared by the game and started barking.

d) The barber complained it was too noisy.

❷ What did some German and British soldiers do during one Christmas week in World War I? Choose *two* answers.

a) They exchanged presents.

b) They continued to fight.

c) They played football in the snow.

d) They cooked a turkey together.

❸ Why were people hurt during the Hillsborough Disaster?

a) There was an earthquake.

b) There was a car crash.

c) There was a tornado.

d) The part of the stadium they were in was overcrowded.

Chapter Two

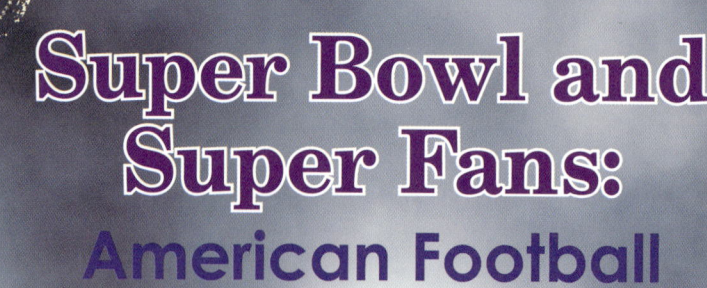

Super Bowl and Super Fans:

American Football

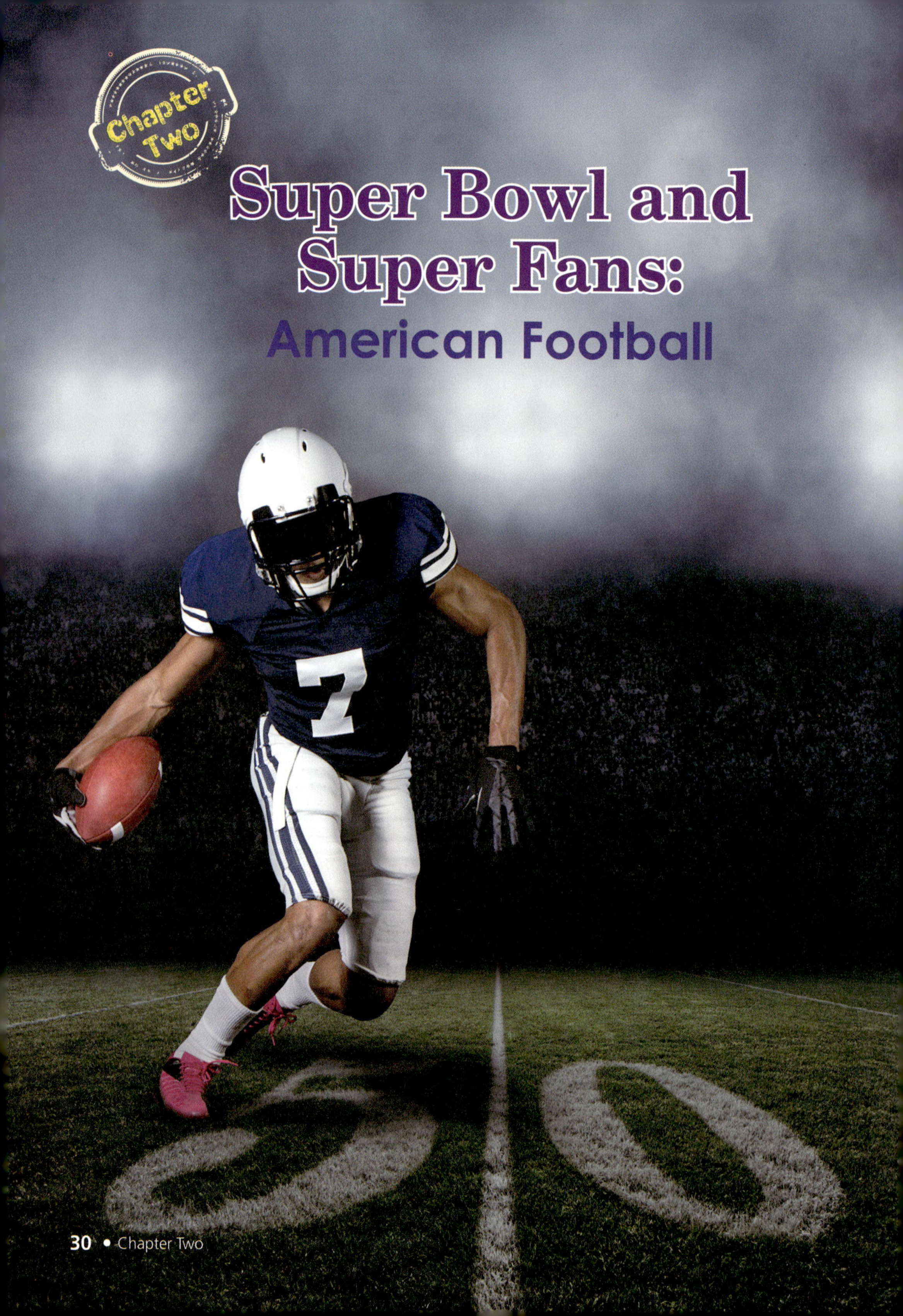

Soccer is not called football in the United States.

The reason is they already had a game called football.

American football is an entirely different sport from soccer.

But it has its roots in soccer and rugby.

It started out as a university game.

The very first American football game was played between Princeton University and Rutgers University in 1869.

But it wasn't until 1880 that the game of American football really took off.

▲ rugby

KEY WORDS

- **super bowl** (*cf.* super)
- **entirely**
- **root**

- **rugby**
- **start out**
- **as**

- **between A and B**
- **until**
- **take off**

▲ Walter Camp
(See page for author
[Public domain or Public domain],
via Wikimedia Commons)

Walter Camp is called the "father" of American football.

He created many of the rules that are used today.

He did that after he played American football as a student at Yale from 1877 to 1882.

He also created the first All-America team.

He chose players that he thought were the best in college American football.

William "Pudge" Heffelfinger was the first American football player who was paid to play.

He received $500 in 1892 to play for a team in New York.

William "Pudge" Heffelfinger ▶
(See page for author [Public domain], via Wikimedia Commons)

KEY WORDS

- from A to B
- **choose** (choose-chose-chosen)
- college
- pudge
- pay

In 1922, the National Football League, the NFL, was formed in the United States with eighteen teams.

Today it has thirty-two teams.

Each team is worth about one billion dollars.

Now that's a lot of money!

About three million people work for the NFL.

The game saw big changes in the 1930s.

The NFL started something new in 1936 called the draft.

Teams chose their players for the next season.

The team that had the lowest number of wins got to choose first.

They still have a draft today.

KEY WORDS

- **National Football League** (*cf.* league)
- worth
- billion
- a lot of

- **see** (see-saw-seen)
- draft
- lowest
- get to + *Verb*

In 1934, they decided to change the shape of the football.

It had been round.

The balls had mostly been made out of bladders from pigs.

Pig bladders made a round shape.

Then, companies started making the balls out of leather from cows.

They gave the balls a smaller middle and pointed ends.

This football was easier to throw and catch. 📖 Aha!

Wilson Sporting Goods is the only company that makes footballs for the NFL.

It makes about four thousand footballs every day.

It takes about 3,000 cow skins to make all of the footballs each year.

However, people still call the footballs "pigskins."

▲ a man making a ball with a pig's bladder
(After Joseph Wright of Derby [Public domain], via Wikimedia Commons)

▲ Richard Lindon who made a leather ball
(See page for author [Public domain or Public domain], via Wikimedia Commons)

(See page for author [Public domain],
via Wikimedia Commons)

Helmets started out as soft leather caps.

In the 1930s, they changed to hard leather.

Now they are made of plastic.

Players attached metal face masks to the hard helmets.

KEY WORDS

- mostly
- be made (out) of
- bladder
- company
- leather
- middle
- pointed

- end
- easier
- throw (throw-threw-thrown)
- catch (catch-caught-caught)
- goods
- skin
- pigskin

- cap
- hard
- plastic
- attach
- metal

Recently, the NFL found out that many former American football players are suffering from head injuries.

In games, hits on the head can cause problems years later.

So new safety rules were written and helmets were improved.

Today's helmets have extra padding and are custom fit to each player.

The quarterback may have a radio in his helmet.

The coach can use the radio to tell him the next play.

If you see a helmet with a green dot on it, it has a radio.

▲ a coach instructing his quarterback through a radio in the player's helmet

Heat stroke is dangerous for players.

Heat stroke happens when a person's body temperature gets too hot.

One way to keep players safe on hot days is the Core Temperature Thermometer Pill.

Today, many players take this pill before a game.

During the game, the pill sends a signal to a trainer.

It tells the trainer the player's body temperature.

If the player gets too hot, he is pulled from the game.

This protects players from heat stroke.

POP QUIZ

What is heat stroke?

ⓐ It is when lightning hits a player.
ⓑ It is when a player's body temperature gets too high.

KEY WORDS

- recently
- find out
- former
- suffer from
- injury
- hit (hit-hit-hit)
- be written
- be improved
- extra
- padding
- custom
- fit
- quarterback
- radio

- coach
- green
- dot
- heat stroke
- dangerous
- happen
- temperature
- Core Temperature Thermometer Pill
  (*cf.* core / thermometer / pill)
- send (send-sent-sent)
- signal
- trainer
- be pulled from
- protect

In 1959, a Texas oilman named Lamar Hunt asked if his team could join the NFL.

They said no because they did not think they needed any more teams.

So Hunt decided to form his own league.

He called it the American Football League, the AFL.

Seven years later, the two leagues decided to join forces.

They thought it would make American football better.

The leagues were renamed the AFC and NFC.

They played separate games until both leagues had a winning team.

Then, they played a Super Bowl game.

KEY WORDS

- oilman
- join
- own
- join forces

- rename
- separate
- both
- call A after B

- according to
- legend
- stand for (stand-stood-stood)
- greatness

▲ the Vince Lombardi Trophy
(By Stephen Luke [CC BY 2.0 (http://
creativecommons.org/licenses/by/2.0)],
via Wikimedia Commons)

The first Super Bowl was played in Los Angeles on January 15, 1967. The Green Bay Packers won. Vince Lombardi was the coach of that team.

Now the Super Bowl Trophy is called the Vince Lombardi Trophy after this great coach.

The Green Bay Packers have the letter G on their helmets. According to legend, the G does not stand for Green.

It stands for Greatness.

the Green Bay Packers' logo G ▶
(By This vector image was first created with Adobe Illustrator by Daris
Bayliss, and then manually edited by Green Bay Packers.
(Green Bay Packers) [Public domain], via Wikimedia Commons)

POP QUIZ

According to legend, what does the letter G on the Green Bay Packers helmet stand for?

ⓐ greatness
ⓑ Green Bay

▲ (By CTLiotta (Own work) [CC0], via Wikimedia Commons)

Over 100 million people watch the Super Bowl each year.
Parties are held all over the United States to watch the
game.

Thanksgiving is the only day when Americans eat more
food than Super Bowl Sunday.

The most popular foods are pizza, chips, and dip. 📖 Aha!

Some fans even start their days with Gronk Flakes.

That's a cereal named after a famous player named Rob
Gronkowski.

American football is the most popular sport in the United States.

However, it has not become as popular in other countries. The International Federation of American Football, IFAF, was formed in 1998.

It wants to make American football an international sport.

Will it happen?

Only time will tell.

POP QUIZ

What does the International Federation of American Football (IFAF) want to do?

ⓐ create a new type of football game
ⓑ make American football an international sport

KEY WORDS

- all over
- Thanksgiving
- chip
- dip
- flake (*cf.* flakes)
- cereal

Comprehension Quiz

A Mark T for true or F for false.

❶ Each NFL football team is worth about
three million dollars.　　　　　　　　　　　T　F

❷ In 1922, the NFL had twenty teams.　　　T　F

❸ The NFL employs about three million people.　T　F

❹ There are thirty-two teams in the NFL today.　T　F

❺ Vince Lombardi was the coach of the first
Super Bowl winning team.　　　　　　　　T　F

B Fill in each blank with the right word below.

universities	rugby	radio	leather

❶ American football has its roots in soccer and ＿＿＿＿＿＿.

❷ American football began as a game between ＿＿＿＿＿＿.

❸ The early football helmets were made of soft ＿＿＿＿＿＿.

❹ A green dot on a football helmet means the helmet has a
＿＿＿＿＿＿ in it.

C Choose the best answer to each question.

❶ What did Walter Camp do for American football? Choose *two* answers.

a) He made players wear helmets.

b) He created many of the rules of the game.

c) He set up the first All-America team.

d) He formed the NFL.

❷ How does the Core Temperature Thermometer Pill work?

a) It lets the trainers see the body temperature of each player.

b) It keeps the players cool when it is hot.

c) It gives the players energy.

d) It tells the players if they are working too hard.

❸ Why did the NFL tell Lamar Hunt he could not add his team to the league?

a) They did not like Lamar Hunt.

b) His team was not good enough to be in the NFL.

c) He did not have enough money to pay the fees.

d) They thought they had enough teams already.

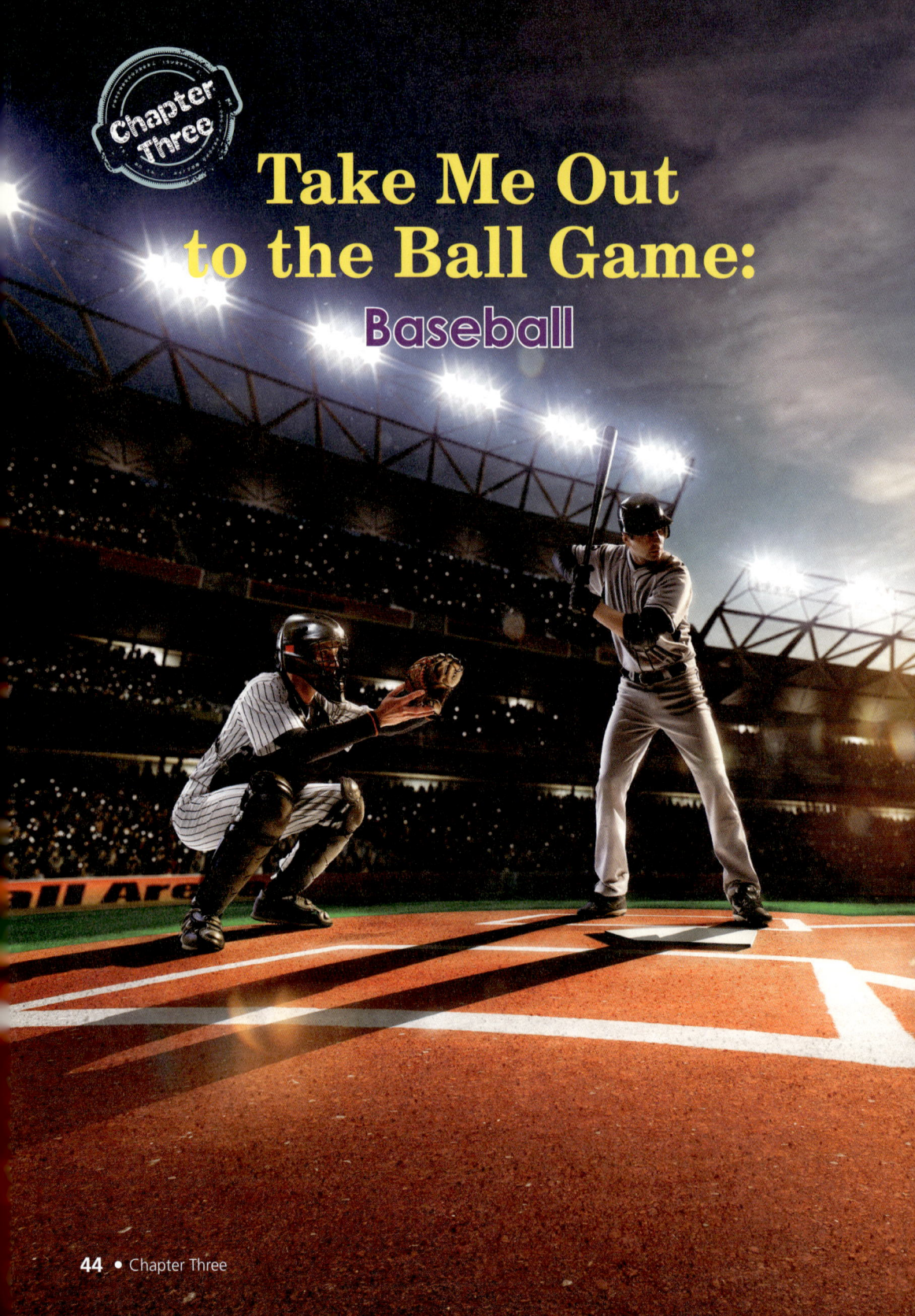

Take Me Out to the Ball Game:
Baseball

The beginning of baseball is shrouded in mystery.

In the United States, there was a rumor that it was created by Abner Doubleday in 1839.

That rumor was proved false.

There were many stick and ball games played in England centuries before that.

Some people think baseball is a form of either cricket or stoolball. 🌐

But it has rules almost like a game called rounders.

Rounders has been played in England since the 1500s.

The game of rounders was sometimes called base ball, with two words.

However the game of baseball began, today it is called "America's Pastime."

KEY WORDS

- take + *Person* + out
- ball game
- shroud
- mystery
- rumor

- be proved (*cf.* prove)
- stick
- either A or B
- cricket
- stoolball

- rounders
- since
- sometimes
- pastime

▲ the New York Knickerbocker Base Ball Club
(See page for author [Public domain], via Wikimedia Commons)

One of the first baseball clubs in America was the New York Knickerbocker Base Ball Club.

They decided to use a diamond-shaped field with foul lines.

They also decided on a rule for batters.

A batter tries to hit the ball.

A miss is called a strike.

He is allowed to miss two times.

But on the third strike he is out.

POP QUIZ

Who decided baseball should be played on a diamond-shaped field?

ⓐ the New York Nine Base Ball Club
ⓑ the New York Knickerbocker Base Ball Club

KEY WORDS

- diamond-shaped
- foul
- batter (*cf.* bat)

- miss
- strike
- third

- be out

One of the earliest games played with these rules was in 1846.

The Knickerbockers played against the New York Nine.

The Knickerbockers lost 23 to 1.

Today's baseball games don't usually have such high scores.

One reason is because the balls are pitched much faster.  Most pitchers throw balls from 130 to 160 kilometers per hour (kph).

That is hard to hit.

The fastest pitch ever by Nolan Ryan was almost 174 kph!

KEY WORDS

- earliest
- usually
- be pitched (*cf.* pitch)

- faster
- pitcher
- per

- kph (= kilometers per hour)
- fastest

The National League was formed with eight professional baseball teams in 1876.

In 1901, the American League was formed with eight more professional teams.

Beginning in 1903, the winning team of each league played in the World Series. 🌐

But the two leagues remained separate until the year 2000. Then, they came together under one league.

They are now both part of Major League Baseball, the MLB.

In the 1870s, a player named A. G. Spalding helped organize the National League. He founded Spalding Sporting Goods.

His company produced baseballs, bats, gloves, uniforms, and caps.

He created the "business of baseball."

▲ A. G. Spalding
(By Boston Red Stockings ([1]) [Public domain], via Wikimedia Commons)

Mr. Spalding was a shrewd businessman.

He wrote a baseball rulebook.

In it, he wrote that the only balls allowed were Spalding baseballs.

KEY WORDS

- National League
- remain
- come together
- under
- major

- organize
- found
- produce
- glove
- uniform

- business
- shrewd
- businessman
- rulebook

Do you think the baseballs used in professional games are clean and smooth?

Think again.

Before a game, the baseballs are rubbed in a special mud.

This special mud is called Baseball Rubbing Mud.

It comes from a secret spot in the Delaware River.

The mud is thick like chocolate pudding.

The umpire or clubhouse attendant rubs mud and water on the balls.

Why do they do this?

It is to take the shine off the baseballs.

This makes them easier for the pitchers to hold and throw.

KEY WORDS

- rub
- mud
- come from
- spot

- thick
- pudding
- umpire
- clubhouse

- attendant
- take the shine off

Some baseball players are as popular as entertainers. Some of them even have things named after them. One of these early players was Cy Young.
He was a pitcher in the early 1900s.
He set records for games won, games pitched, and innings pitched.
His records have never been broken.
Today, the Cy Young Award is given each year to the best pitcher.

▲ Cy Young
(By Charles M. Conlon (Mears Auctions)
[Public domain], via Wikimedia Commons)

KEY WORDS

• entertainer
• **set a record** (set-set-set)(*cf.* record)

• inning
• award

Take Me Out to the Ball Game: Baseball • **51**

One of the most famous batters of all time was George Herman Ruth.

Some people call him Babe Ruth or simply "The Babe."

He hit more home runs than any other player of his time.

In 1923, the New York Yankees built a new stadium.

Babe Ruth stepped up to the plate.

He hit a home run at his first at bat.

After that, they nicknamed the stadium "The House that Ruth Built."

Babe Ruth set a record of 714 home runs.

It was not broken for many years.

POP QUIZ

What stadium is called "The House that Ruth Built?"

ⓐ Yankee Stadium
ⓑ Dodger Stadium

KEY WORDS

- of all time
- babe
- simply

- home run
- step up to
- plate

- at bat
- nickname

Yours Truly
"Babe Ruth"

© I·L·P
#6

▲ Babe Ruth
(By Irwin, La Broad, & Pudlin.
[Public domain],
via Wikimedia Commons)

Lou "Buster" Gehrig ▶
(By Pacific & Atlantic Photos,
Inc (Heritage Auctions) [Public domain],
via Wikimedia Commons)

Lou "Buster" Gehrig loved playing baseball.

This first baseman never wanted to miss a game.

He would come to a game even if he was sick.

He set a record for the most consecutive games played.

He played 2,130 games in a row!

However, he began to make little mistakes.

Sometimes he dropped the ball.

He even stumbled and fell.

A disease was making his muscles weak.

It was called ALS.

The disease is now called Lou Gehrig's Disease.

In 1939, he had to retire.

Even though he was dying, Lou Gehrig was grateful for his fans.

In his farewell speech at Yankee Stadium he said, "Today I consider myself the luckiest man on the face of the earth."

KEY WORDS

- baseman
- even if
- consecutive
- in a row
- drop
- stumble
- disease
- muscle
- ALS (= amyotrophic lateral sclerosis)
- retire
- even though
- be grateful for
- farewell speech
- consider
- on the face of the earth

▲ Jackie Robinson
(By United States Information Agency
[Public domain], via Wikimedia Commons)

At one time, African Americans were not allowed to play in the professional leagues.
This didn't stop Jackie Robinson.
In 1947, he joined the Brooklyn Dodgers.
When he came onto the field, the crowd booed and threw trash at him.
But he stayed strong.

He didn't fight back.
He stood up for what is right.

POP QUIZ

Why did some people think Jackie Robinson should not play professional baseball?

ⓐ Jackie Robinson was an African American.
ⓑ Jackie Robinson was not a good hitter.

KEY WORDS

- at one time
- African American
- boo
- trash

- stay strong
- fight back (fight-fought-fought)
- stand up for

Jackie won the Rookie of the Year Award in 1947 and the Most Valuable Player (MVP) Award in 1949.

He was the first African American to win those awards.

He also played in six World Series.

Today, Jackie Robinson is one of the most famous players of all time.

He helped make it possible for anyone to play baseball.

April 15 of each year is now celebrated as Jackie Robinson Day in the USA.

On that day, all the professional players wear uniforms with the number 42 on them.

That was Jackie's number.

▲ Jackie Robinson's uniform number, 42, being displayed at the Jackie Robinson Rotunda, a memorial for him
(By Jtesla16 (Own work) [CC BY 3.0 (http://creativecommons.org/licenses/by/3.0)], via Wikimedia Commons)

KEY WORDS

- rookie
- valuable
- possible
- **wear** (wear-wore-worn)

Hank Aaron started playing for the Milwaukee Braves in 1954.

He was also an African American.

Some people still didn't think black people should play baseball.

But like Jackie, he didn't let that stop him.

He never got mad, even when white people sent him hate mail.

In fact, it was so bad that sometimes he had to have a guard with him when he came to the games.

On April 8, 1974, Hank Aaron hit home run number 715.

That broke Babe Ruth's record.

The crowd in Atlanta, Georgia roared as the ball sailed over the wall of the left outfield.

By the end of his baseball career, he had hit 755 home runs.

This record was not broken for 30 years.

KEY WORDS

- get mad
- hate mail
- in fact

- guard
- roar
- sail over the wall

- outfield
- by the end of
- career

▲ Hank Aaron

(By Lauren Gerson [Public domain], via Wikimedia Commons)

Hank Aaron's Hall of Fame plaque ▶

(By User:Alkivar (Wikipedia)

[Copyrighted free use or Public domain],

via Wikimedia Commons)

▲ Yogi Berra
(By Bowman Gum (Heritage Auctions)
[Public domain], via Wikimedia Commons)

Some popular sayings came from baseball.

Yogi Berra is famous for the saying, "It ain't over till it's over." 🌐

His team, the New York Mets, was losing the division title against the Chicago Cubs.

They were almost ten games behind.

Yogi said, "It ain't over till it's over."

He was proved right.

The Mets came back to win the division title.

They went on to play in the World Series.

KEY WORDS

- saying
- be famous for
- ain't
- be over

- till
- division
- title
- cub

- behind
- go on to + *Verb*

A well-known baseball song is "Take Me Out to the Ball Game." 🌐

It's played at many ball games in the middle of the seventh inning.

In 2001, Nike made a commercial.

Baseball players sang parts of the song in their native languages.

Ken Griffey Jr. sang in English.

Park Chan Ho sang in Korean.

Alex Rodriguez sang in Spanish.

Kazuhiro Sasaki sang in Japanese.

Wherever you are in the world, you can sing along to "Take Me Out to the Ball Game."

Comprehension Quiz

A Solve the crossword puzzle.

Across

❹ Baseball has rules similar to the game _____.

Down

❶ A baseball field is shaped like a _____.

❷ Rubbing mud looks like chocolate _____.

❸ Three _____ and the player is out.

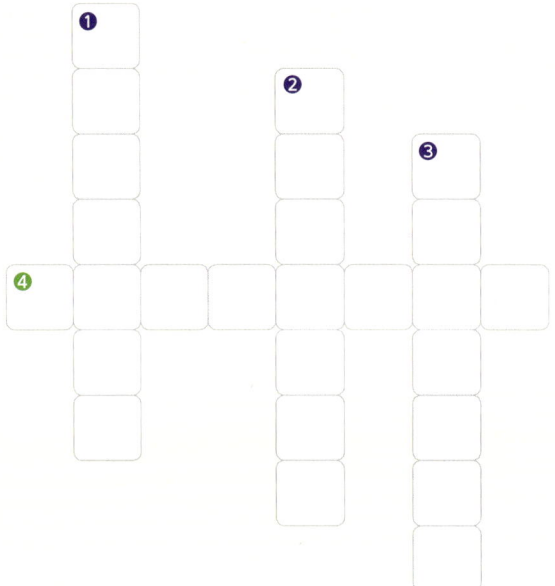

B Choose the best answer to each question.

❶ Why is it so hard to determine when and how baseball began?

a) Records from ancient China have been lost.

b) No one wrote down baseball history.

c) There have been so many different stick and ball games.

d) Early baseball records were burned in a fire.

❷ What is one reason baseball games don't have very high scores?

a) Not much happens in baseball.

b) The rules are too strict.

c) The players are not as good as football players.

d) Balls are pitched very fast.

❸ What is Lou Gehrig most famous for doing?

a) He broke Babe Ruth's home run record.

b) He was the first African-American baseball player.

c) He caught the most fly balls in history.

d) He played in 2,130 consecutive games.

From Peach Baskets to Hoop Shots:
Basketball

Dr. James Naismith was a teacher at a YMCA training school.

He taught physical fitness.

In 1891, it was a cold winter in Springfield, Massachusetts.

That created a problem.

It was too cold to exercise outside.

Naismith needed to find a fun activity that the men could play indoors.

He hung peach baskets at both ends of a gymnasium.
Then he picked up a soccer ball.
He tried to shoot the ball into the baskets.
The game of basketball was born.
It quickly became popular.
In fifteen years, basketball was played around the world.
In 1906, they changed from peach baskets to basketball hoops.
By the 1940s, basketball in the USA had a professional men's league.
It was called the National Basketball Association, or simply the NBA.

▲ the first basketball court with a peach basket on the wall
(By The original uploader was Kinston eagle at English Wikipedia [Public domain], via Wikimedia Commons)

KEY WORDS

- peach
- hoop shot (*cf.* hoop / shot)
- YMCA
- training
- physical fitness
- too + *Adjective/Adverb* + to + *Verb*
- exercise

- activity
- hang (hang-hung-hung)
- gymnasium
- pick up (*cf.* pick)
- shoot (shoot-shot-shot)
- National Basketball Association

▲ (By Hatmatbbat10 (Own work) [Public domain], via Wikimedia Commons)

Do you remember A. G. Spalding, the man who created the "business of baseball?"

In 1894, he developed the first basketball.

His company now makes the official NBA basketballs.

It also makes the official NBA backboards.

In fact, Spalding® is the world's largest basketball equipment supplier.

Perhaps you can say Mr. Spalding also created the "business of basketball."

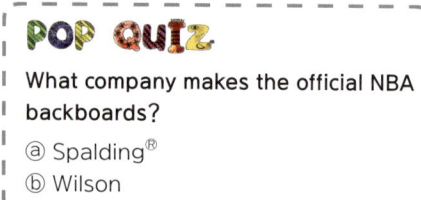

POP QUIZ

What company makes the official NBA backboards?

ⓐ Spalding®
ⓑ Wilson

KEY WORDS

- develop
- backboard
- Ⓡ (= registered trademark)
- equipment

- supplier
- introduce
- limit
- certain

- be reached (*cf.* reach)
- a free throw

Before 1954, the game was much slower than it is today.
But a man named Daniel Biasone changed that.
He introduced two new things.
The team foul limit was one change.
This meant a team was only allowed a certain number of team fouls.
After the limit was reached, the other team got a free throw shot.

▼ a player shooting a free throw and other players around him

Another change was the shot clock.

Biasone wanted the pro game to have a 24-second shot clock.

This meant that when a team had the ball, they had to shoot for a basket within 24 seconds.

If they didn't, they had to give the ball to the other team.

This made teams work harder to score faster. 📖 Aha!

Biasone was inducted into the Basketball Hall of Fame for introducing the use of the 24-second shot clock.

▲ Naismith Memorial Basketball Hall of Fame

KEY WORDS

- shot clock
- pro (= professional)
- within
- induct
- the hall of fame

Before this, the average score in a game was around 80. After these two changes, the scores of basketball games started going higher than 100 points.

But no one expected one person to score 100 points in one game.

That's what happened in 1962. Wilt Chamberlain was one of basketball's superstars.

In a famous game between the Warriors and the Knicks, Wilt scored 100 points all by himself.

It is remembered as the "100-point game." This record has never been broken.

▲ a game between the Philadelphia Warriors and the New York Knicks
(See page for author [Public domain], via Wikimedia Commons)

KEY WORDS

- average
- around
- point
- expect
- superstar
- (all) by oneself

▲ Wilt Chamberlain holding a ball during the game
(By New York World-Telegram and the Sun staff
photographer [Public domain], via Wikimedia Commons)

At more than two meters tall, Wilt Chamberlain towered over other players. He had several nicknames. He was called "The Big Dipper." It's because he was so tall he had to "dip" his head to get through doorways. Some called him "Wilt the Stilt." Other fans called him "Goliath."

He played for the Harlem Globetrotters in 1958 and 1959.

Then, he started playing for the Philadelphia Warriors.

He was the NBA Rookie of the Year in 1960.

He was named an All-Star thirteen times.

He was the NBA Scoring Champion seven times.

He was the Most Valuable Player (MVP) five times.

POP QUIZ

How many times did Wilt Chamberlain win the MVP award?

ⓐ five　　　　　　　　ⓑ thirteen

Michael Jordan had a big impact on the sport.

At first, people didn't think he could be a good basketball player.

He wanted to play on his high school varsity basketball team.

He didn't get picked.

The coaches thought he was too short.

So he played junior varsity.

He practiced extra hours every day.

He worked hard to improve his shot.

When he grew taller, he joined the varsity team.

▲ Michael Jordan
(Steve Lipofsky at basketballphoto.com [GFDL (http://www.gnu.org/copyleft/fdl.html) or CC-BY-SA-3.0 (http://creativecommons.org/licenses/by-sa/3.0/)], via Wikimedia Commons)

KEY WORDS

- **meter** $(1\,m = 100\,cm)$
- **tower**
- **big dipper**
- **dip**
- **get through**

- **doorway**
- **stilt**
- **Goliath**
- **Harlem**
- **all-star**

- **have an impact on** (*cf*. impact)
- **at first**
- **varsity**
- **junior varsity**
- **grow** (grow-grew-grown)

In 1984, Jordan was passed over in the draft by the Portland Trail Blazers. 📖 Aha!

He signed with the Chicago Bulls.

He was the NBA Rookie of the Year.

He set many more records.

He won many more awards.

In 1999 ESPN, a global sports broadcasting network, named him the Greatest North American Athlete of the Century.

He is in the Basketball Hall of Fame.

Some people say the worst draft decision ever made was when Portland passed over Michael Jordan.

KEY WORDS

- pass + *Person* + over
- sign
- many more
- global
- broadcasting

- network
- greatest
- athlete
- worst
- decision

- sign a deal
- market
- brand
- fine
- finally

Jordan signed a deal with Nike to market his own brand of athletic shoes.

They are called Air Jordans.

When he wore them on the basketball court, the NBA fined him.

Nike paid the fine.

This happened again and again.

Finally, the NBA decided to allow players to wear Air Jordans.

Many other products are now part of the Jordan brand.

After he retired from basketball, Jordan became part owner of a basketball team. It was the Charlotte Bobcats.

Now he is one of the richest men in the world.

He was the first NBA player to become a billionaire.

He achieved all of this because he didn't give up.

When the high school coaches didn't pick him, he worked harder to reach his dream.

He is quoted as saying, "Obstacles don't have to stop you. If you run into a wall, don't turn around and give up. Figure out how to climb it, go through it, or work around it."

KEY WORDS

- part owner
- richest
- billionaire
- achieve
- **give up** (give-gave-given)

- quote
- obstacle
- run into
- turn around
- figure out

- climb
- go through
- work around

The Harlem
Globetrotters is a
basketball team
that doesn't believe
in obstacles.
The players
entertain crowds
with fancy tricks.
They have some
funny nicknames.

▲ Harlem Globetrotters
(By CBS Television (eBay item photo front photo back)
[Public domain], via Wikimedia Commons)

Jonte "Too Tall" Hall is the shortest Globetrotter ever.

Paul "Tiny" Sturgis is the tallest player ever.

Another player was named "Super" Mario Green.

POP QUIZ

Who is the shortest Harlem Globetrotter?
ⓐ Jonte "Too Tall" Hall
ⓑ Paul "Tiny" Sturgis

KEY WORDS
- believe in
- entertain
- fancy
- trick
- tiny

Corey "Thunder" Law once made a hoop shot blindfolded.
He did this from over twenty-one meters away!
He could also shoot backwards, without looking at the hoop.
His longest backward shot was twenty-five meters!
In 2013, he shot a hoop from 33.45 meters away!
Crowds love to see the tricks the players can do with the basketball.
Today's hoop shots have come a long way from the peach baskets in Springfield, Massachusetts.

POP QUIZ

Which Harlem Globetrotter once made a hoop shot wearing a blindfold?

ⓐ Wilt Chamberlain
ⓑ Corey "Thunder" Law

KEY WORDS

- once
- make a shot
- blindfolded
- backwards (*cf.* backward)
- come a long way

Chapter Four

Comprehension Quiz

A Mark T for true or F for false.

❶ The inventor of basketball taught physical education. T F

❷ Peach baskets and baseballs were used in the first basketball games. T F

❸ Spalding Sporting Goods created the first official basketball. T F

B Fill in each blank with the right word below.

faster	ball	hoops	businessman

❶ They changed from peach baskets to basketball _____ in 1906.

❷ The shot clock made the game _____ and higher scoring.

❸ In addition to being a great basketball player, Michael Jordan is a smart _____.

❹ If a team doesn't try to shoot a hoop within 24 seconds, the other team gets the _____.

C Choose the best answer to each question.

❶ What two things did Biasone introduce to the game of basketball?

a) the team foul limit and the foul line

b) the shot clock and the team foul limit

c) the shot clock and the dunk shot

d) the foul limit and the dunk shot

❷ Why didn't Michael Jordan get picked for his high school varsity basketball team?

a) He couldn't play basketball very well.

b) He was better at baseball.

c) The coaches thought he was too short.

d) His school didn't have a varsity team.

❸ What happened the first time Jordan wore his Air Jordan shoes on the basketball court?

a) His coach made him take them off.

b) The other players wanted to buy the shoes.

c) He sold them to fans after the game.

d) The NBA fined him and Nike paid the fine.

To the Moon and Back:
Golf

It has been played on the sides of volcanoes.

It has been played in ice and snow.

It has even been played on the moon.

What sport is it?

It is golf.

The game of golf is many centuries old.

Some pictures of ancient times in China show a game called Chuiwan.

They show people hitting balls with sticks.

There are ancient Chinese writings about it, too.

It was played as far back as the Tang Dynasty.

The rules were almost like modern golf.

Players used up to ten different clubs.

They hit wooden balls into holes.

Players had to be good sports.

They had to use good manners when they played.

Golf is still like that today.

▲ a picture showing people playing a game similar to golf In ancient China
(By English: en:Shang Xi, Chinese imperial court painter in the 15th century Čeština:
Šang Si, čínský malíř pracující u císařského dvora, tvořil ve 30. letech 15. století
(www.spiegel.de) [Public domain], via Wikimedia Commons)

KEY WORDS

- to the moon and back
- volcano
- ancient times (*cf.* ancient)
- writing
- far back
- **Tang Dynasty** (*cf.* dynasty)
- wooden
- be a good sport
- **manners** (*cf.* manner)

A picture from an ancient tomb in Egypt shows a game similar to golf.

The tomb is 2,600 years old.

Historians think ancient Rome and Greece had a game like golf, too.

Long ago in Scotland, King James II didn't want his soldiers to play golf.

He thought they would spend their time playing golf instead of practicing with their bows and arrows.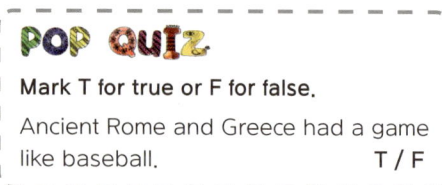

So in 1457, he banned the game.

He also banned soccer for the same reason.

POP QUIZ

Mark T for true or F for false.

Ancient Rome and Greece had a game like baseball.　　　　T / F

KEY WORDS

- tomb
- similar to
- long ago
- instead of
- bow

- arrow
- disappear
- lift the ban
- Queen of Scots
- cadet

- carry
- term
- caddy

Golf was banned for many years, but it didn't disappear.

King James IV started to play it.

In 1502, he lifted the ban.

Later, Mary Queen of Scots played the game.

She had her cadets carry her golf clubs for her.

It is said that is where we get the term caddy.

St. Andrews University taught students golf as far back as the 1400s.

That is why many people call St. Andrews "the cradle of golf."

Back then, there were no golf courses like we have today.

St. Andrews Royal and Ancient Club was founded in 1754. It had a twelve-hole course.

Since then, golf courses have been built all over the world. Some are in exotic places.

▲ the world's oldest golf course St. Andrews

KEY WORDS

- cradle
- golf course
- all over the world
- exotic

The Lost City Golf Course in Sun City, South Africa is unusual.

On the 13th hole, there is a water hazard with Nile crocodiles!

The Elephant Hills Golf Course is in Zimbabwe.

On this course, golfers can see African wildlife when they tee off.

What about golfing next to a volcano?

There are many to choose from in South America.

The Fuego Maya Golf Course in Guatemala lies between two volcanoes.

18 holes golf course

KEY WORDS

- unusual
- water hazard
- crocodile
- Zimbabwe
- golfer
- wildlife
- tee off (*cf.* tee)
- what about ~?
- next to
- lie (lie-lay-lain)

Bangkok is famous for its Kantarat Golf Course.

It lies between two runways at an airport.

A red light stops the golfers when a plane approaches.

In Greenland, there is a golf course on a glacier.

Players use red or orange balls so they can see them in the snow.

In Idaho, there is a golf course with a floating green.

The Floating Green is a man-made island that moves.

The golfers hit from the shore of a lake to the island.

If they miss, their balls end up at the bottom of the lake.

The astronaut Alan Shepard hit some golf balls on the moon.

He played with one hand because his space suit was stiff.

No one knows how far those golf balls went.

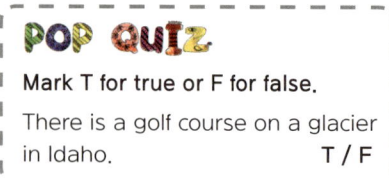

POP QUIZ

Mark T for true or F for false.

There is a golf course on a glacier in Idaho.   T / F

KEY WORDS

- runway
- approach
- glacier
- floating

- man-made
- shore
- end up
- at the bottom of

- astronaut
- space suit
- stiff

Some of the first golf balls were made of wood.

▲ featheries
(By Geni (Photo by user:geni) [GFDL
(http://www.gnu.org/copyleft/fdl.html) or
CC BY-SA 4.0-3.0-2.5-2.0-1.0 (http://creativecommons.org/
licenses/by-sa/4.0-3.0-2.5-2.0-1.0)], via Wikimedia Commons)

Others were made of leather and feathers.
These were called featheries.
Three pieces of leather were sewn into a round shape.
It was stuffed with feathers.
This type of ball took a long time to make.
They were very expensive.
That is why most of the first golfers were rich.
Poor people couldn't afford to buy the balls.

KEY WORDS

- feather
- sew (sew-sewed-sewn/sewed)
- be stuffed with

- expensive
- afford to + *Verb*

In 1848, a man created the first rubber golf ball.

He used gutta-percha gum from the Gutta tree.

The balls were called gutties.

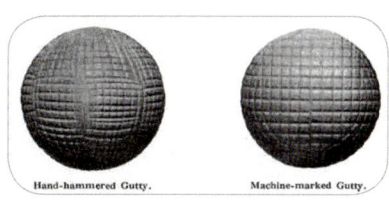

▲ gutties
([Public domain], via Wikimedia Commons)

They were painted white in the summer so they could be seen in the grass.

They were red in the winter to be seen in the snow.

Fast forward fifty years to 1898.

Coburn Haskell found a new way to make golf balls.

The new Haskell ball could be made in factories.

It was cheaper than the old gutties.

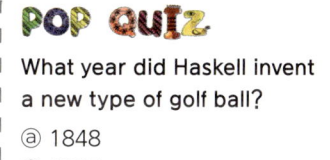

POP QUIZ

What year did Haskell invent
a new type of golf ball?

ⓐ 1848
ⓑ 1898

KEY WORDS

- rubber
- gutta-percha

- gum
- forward

- factory
- cheaper

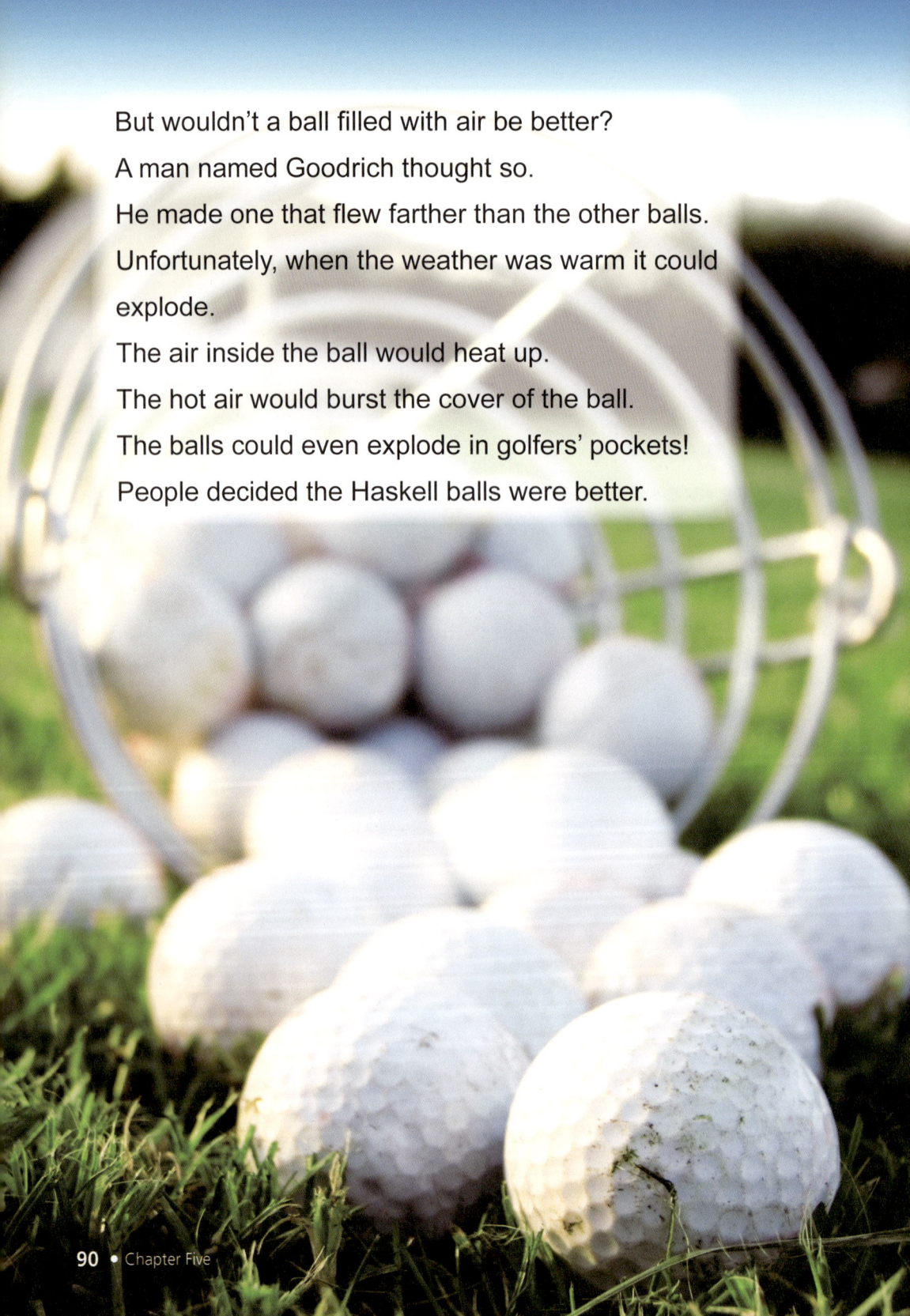

But wouldn't a ball filled with air be better?

A man named Goodrich thought so.

He made one that flew farther than the other balls.

Unfortunately, when the weather was warm it could explode.

The air inside the ball would heat up.

The hot air would burst the cover of the ball.

The balls could even explode in golfers' pockets!

People decided the Haskell balls were better.

The first golf clubs were made of hard
wood.
Some clubs had iron or bone on them
to make them stronger.
But they broke easily.
Today's clubs are lighter.
They can hit the ball farther.
They are made of newer materials,
like graphite.
But they are still called woods and irons.
Golfers hope that with skill and good clubs, they will be
lucky and hit a hole in one.

In most countries, when a golfer hits a hole in one, the other players congratulate him.

But in Japan and Korea, it is different.

When a golfer hits a hole in one, he must throw a party for his friends. 📖 Aha!

These parties can be very expensive.

There are many gifts to give.

Golfers in Japan buy hole-in-one insurance to pay for the party.

If the golfer does not have insurance, it can be very unlucky to hit a hole in one!

POP QUIz

Why do some golfers buy hole-in-one insurance?

ⓐ to make sure they are able to hit a hole in one

ⓑ to pay for the party and gifts if they hit a hole in one

KEY WORDS

- congratulate
- throw a party
- buy an insurance (buy-bought-bought)

- unlucky (↔ lucky)
- Grand Slam

Bobby Jones was one of the first great athletes in modern golf.

He hit many holes in one.

He is the only player to ever win a Grand Slam in one season. 🌐

A Grand Slam happens when a player wins four major tournaments.

Another great golfer was Jack Nicklaus.

He won 18 major tournaments.

▲ Bobby Jones
(By unattributed (Heritage Auctions)
[Public domain], via Wikimedia Commons)

In the 1990s, a new star appeared on the golf scene.

Tiger Woods was on the Mike Douglas television show when he was only two years old.

He showed the audience that he could already hit a golf ball.

He hit his first hole in one when he was eight years old.

Tiger is the winner of 14 major tournaments.

He is tied with Nicklaus with three Career Grand Slams.

Tiger Woods is a top money maker in golf.

▲ Tiger Woods
(By James Phelps (Flickr) [CC BY 2.0
(http://creativecommons.org/licenses/
by/2.0)], via Wikimedia Commons)

Whether it is a goal, a run, or a hole in one, ball games are loved around the world.

KEY WORDS

- **appear** (↔ disappear)
- **scene**
- **audience**

- **winner**
- **tie with**
- **Career Grand Slam**

- **top money maker**
- **whether**
- **run**

Comprehension Quiz

A Mark T for true or F for false.

❶ The name of the game played in ancient China that was similar to golf was Cuju. T F

❷ Featheries were so expensive because they were hand sewn and stuffed. T F

❸ Tiger Woods is the only golfer to win a Grand Slam in one season. T F

❹ There are crocodiles in the water hazard at the Lost City Golf Course. T F

B Fill in each blank with the right word(s) below.

| leather | moon | gutties | airport runways |

❶ The Kantarat Golf Course is between two _____.

❷ Alan Shepard played golf on the _____.

❸ Featheries were made of _____ and feathers.

❹ The first rubber golf balls were called _____.

C Choose the best answer to each question.

❶ Why didn't King James II want his soldiers to play golf?

a) He didn't want them to be better at golf than him.

b) He wanted them to practice riding horses.

c) He wanted them to practice with their bows and arrows.

d) He wanted them to play soccer.

❷ Why are some golf balls colored red or orange?

a) So golfers can see them in the snow.

b) Golfers want some variety.

c) Only the balls for miniature golf are colored.

d) So birds won't think they are eggs.

❸ What is one reason golf clubs are called woods and irons?

a) The first clubs were made of wood and iron.

b) Wood is for soft hits and iron is for harder hits.

c) Irons were used for getting golf balls out of the woods.

d) They made clubs with the wood from the Gutta tree.

Let's Review the Story

Fill in the blanks to review the story.

Title: The World's Most _____

Soccer:
- A game like soccer was played in ancient C____.
- Soccer went from E_____ to other countries.
- The W____ C____ was created by Jules Rimet, the FIFA president.

American Football:
- In 1959, Lamar Hunt formed a new football league, the A_____ F_____ L_____ (AFL).
- In 1967, the first S____ B____ was played.

Baseball:
- B____ R____ hit 714 home runs.
- H____ A____ hit 755 home runs.
- Yogi Berra said, "It ain't _____ till it's _____."

Basketball:
- Basketball is played with a shot _____ and a team foul limit.
- M____ J____ wore Air Jordan shoes on the basketball court.
- Wilt Chamberlain scored _____ points in a game.

Golf:
- In ancient China, a game similar to golf was called C____.
- St. Andrews is called "the c____ of golf."
- Some of the best golfers have won more than one G____ S____.

Let's Think & Talk

Think about the following questions and answer them freely.

❶ Among the ball sports in the book, which is your favorite ball sport? Why?

❷ Besides the ball sports in the book, what other ball sports are there and what are some interesting stories related to those sports? Search for information and stories about them and prepare to tell your friends what you found out.

❸ Among the various ball sports, which ball sport do you want to learn to play? Tell your friends what ball sport it is and why you want to learn to play it.

❹ Who is your favorite sports star? Tell your friends who your favorite player is and the reason he/she is your favorite player.

Answers

Let's Review the Story

Title: The World's Most [Popular Sports]

Soccer:
- A game like soccer was played in ancient [China].
- Soccer went from [England] to other countries.
- The [World] [Cup] was created by Jules Rimet, the FIFA president.

American Football:
- In 1959, Lamar Hunt formed a new football league, the [American] [Football] [League] (AFL).
- In 1967, the first [Super] [Bowl] was played.

Baseball:
- [Babe] [Ruth] hit 714 home runs.
- [Hank] [Aaron] hit 755 home runs.
- Yogi Berra said, "It ain't [over] till it's [over]."

Basketball:
- Basketball is played with a shot [clock] and a team foul limit.
- [Michael] [Jordan] wore Air Jordan shoes on the basketball court.
- Wilt Chamberlain scored [100] points in a game.

Golf:
- In ancient China, a game similar to golf was called [Chuiwan].
- St. Andrews is called "the [cradle] of golf."
- Some of the best golfers have won more than one [Grand] [Slam].

Smart Readers: **Wise** & **Wide**

After-reading Test

- The World's Most Popular Sports
- Level 4
- 27 Questions

(Vocabulary 7 / Reading Comprehension 16 /

Sentence Structure & Grammar 4)

The World's Most Popular Sports After-reading Test

1. Who are "peasants"?
   ① upper class people
   ② working class people
   ③ royal people
   ④ people who make football rules

2. Which of the following is the wrong past tense form of the verb?
   ① hit − hit
   ② set − set
   ③ sew − sew
   ④ spread − spread

3. Which of the following is the wrong superlative form of the adjective?
   ① fast → fastest
   ② rich → richest
   ③ large → largest
   ④ early → earlyest

※ Choose the right word for each blank. (4~5)

4.
   They had mostly been made _____ of bladders from pigs.

   ① like   ② out
   ③ to   ④ off

5.

> They went _____ to play in the World Series.

① on   ② in

③ at   ④ toward

※ Choose the common word for the two blanks. (6~7)

6.

> • One reason Brazil won so many World Cups was due _____
>   a tremendous player.
> • A picture from an ancient tomb in Egypt shows a game similar
>   _____ golf.

① to   ② for

③ of   ④ with

7.

> • It was stuffed _____ feathers.
> • He is tied _____ Nicklaus with three Career Grand Slams.

① of   ② on

③ with   ④ against

※ Choose the right answer to each question about soccer. (8~10)

8. In the game in ancient China, what did the square court and round ball represent?

① yin and yang

② sky and trees

③ spirit and earth

④ good and evil

9. When Pelé went to Nigeria to play a game during a war, what did the soldiers do?
   ① They stopped fighting to watch the game.
   ② They left the country.
   ③ They sent tickets to their families.
   ④ They told Pelé it was too dangerous to come to Nigeria.

10. Why was FIFA formed?
   ① to make a big company to run football games
   ② to help football players from poor countries
   ③ to form an international organization to make rules
   ④ to raise money to build football stadiums

※ Choose the right answer to each question about American football. (11~13)
11. How do coaches use helmet radios?
   ① They play music for the football players.
   ② They let the football players get phone calls from fans.
   ③ They talk with the referees during the games.
   ④ They tell the players what plays to run.

12. What is the Super Bowl?
   ① a game played between the best teams of the AFC and the NFC
   ② a game played at the World Cup
   ③ a big stadium for American football games
   ④ a game played between the best players from every team in the NFL

13. How dangerous are head injuries in American football?
   ① Not very dangerous, because the helmets protect the players.
   ② Very dangerous, because the injuries can affect the players years later.
   ③ Not dangerous if a doctor treats them right away.
   ④ Only dangerous if the player gets his helmet knocked off.

※ Choose the right answer to each question about baseball. (14~17)
14. What is the World Series?
   ① a tournament involving the seven best MLB teams
   ② a game between teams from different countries
   ③ a series of games between the American League and the National League winning teams
   ④ a game between the AFC and NFC champions

15. What does baseball rubbing mud do?
   ① It makes baseballs look brown and dirty.
   ② It makes the catcher's glove sticky.
   ③ It colors the dirt on the pitcher's mound.
   ④ It takes the shine off of new baseballs.

16. What did the disease ALS do to Lou Gehrig?
   ① It made him angry.
   ② It made his muscles weak.
   ③ It made him fat.
   ④ It made him forget things.

17. What do baseball players do on April 15 of each year?

① They pay taxes.

② They sign baseball cards for children.

③ They boycott baseball games.

④ They wear the number 42 on their uniforms to honor Jackie Robinson.

※ Choose the right answer to each question about basketball. (18~20)

18. What is the professional shot clock rule?

① The team that has the ball must shoot within twenty-four seconds.

② The team with the ball must not keep it more than two minutes.

③ The team which is fouled gets an extra shot.

④ The team gets an extra four points if they score before the clock rings.

19. What does "the 100-point game" refer to?

① the first game a team scored 100 points or over in

② the game in which Wilt Chamberlain scored 100 points all by himself

③ the most points a team can score in one game

④ the highest scoring game before the shot clock was introduced

20. Who said, "If you run into a wall, don't turn around and give up?"

① Wilt Chamberlain

② Naismith

③ Michael Jordan

④ Corey "Thunder" Law

※ Choose the right answer to each question about golf. (21~23)

21. Where is the ancient tomb that has pictures of a game similar to golf?

① Egypt

② Rome

③ Greece

④ China

22. What happened to the Goodrich golf balls?

① They became the most popular golf balls of all time.

② People hit them so far they lost them all the time.

③ They sometimes exploded.

④ They were too heavy and they didn't go far.

23. Where can it be considered unlucky to hit a hole in one?

① Japan

② Bangkok

③ Lost City Golf Course

④ United States

※ Choose the wrong part of each sentence. (24~25)

24.
It was enough big to hold 160,000 people.
　①　　　②　　　③　　　④

25.

When a golfer <u>hits</u> a hole <u>in one</u>, he <u>must throws</u> a party for his friends.
    ①   ②   ③   ④

26. Which of the following is the correct word for the blank?

One reason is because the balls are pitched _____ faster.

① too   ② very

③ more   ④ much

27. Which of the following is the correct sentence?

① He thought they would spend their time playing golf.

② He thought they would spend their time play golf.

③ He thought they will spend their time to play golf.

④ He thought they will spend their time to playing golf.

Suzanne Pitner

Suzanne Pitner is a teacher and writer who has enjoyed visiting Alaska, exploring Rome, teaching in China, and is looking forward to more world travel. She has a Master's Degree in Education, and is a graduate of the Long Ridge Writer's Group. In addition to writing educational articles and books, she writes historical fiction and contemporary fiction for young adults using the pen name Suzanne Lilly.

 **Smart Readers Wise & Wide 4-10**

The World's Most Popular Sports

Written by Suzanne Pitner
Illustrated by Yeonjo Kim

First Published in June 2017

Editorial Manager: Juyon Choi
Editors: Kyunghee Jang, Jiyeong Park
Designer: Eunhee Lee
Cover Designer: Eunhee Lee

Published and distributed by

 Happy House

Darakwon Bldg., 64-1 Jandari-ro, Mapo-gu, Seoul, Korea 04031
Tel: 82-2-736-2031(ext. 250)   Fax: 82-2-732-2037
Homepage: www.ihappyhouse.co.kr
Publisher: Kyudo Chung

ISBN: 978-89-6653-536-1 18740 / 978-89-6653-156-1 18740(set)

[Components]
• 1 Audio CD (Recording Studio: Aram)
• Answer Keys & Korean Translation: Free download at www.ihappyhouse.co.kr